Table of Contents

I0442205

Media coverage of any future operation will, to a large extent, shape public perception of the national security environment now and in the years ahead. This holds true for the US public; the public in allied countries whose opinion can affect the durability of our coalition; and publics in countries where we conduct operations, whose perceptions of us can affect the cost and duration of our involvement. Our ultimate strategic success in bringing peace and security to this region will come in our long-term commitment to supporting our democratic ideals. We need to tell the factual story – good or bad – before others seed the media with disinformation and distortions, as they most certainly will continue to do.

US Secretary of Defense Donald Rumsfeld

INTRODUCTION

The law of armed conflict requires combatants to distinguish between the civilian population and civilian objects, and military objectives, with attacks only permitted against the latter. Discerning what constitutes a legitimate military target, however, becomes more difficult when objects are used for both civilian and military purposes. This article examines one such "dual use," that of the media during the combat operations phase of Operation IRAQI FREEDOM (OIF).[1]

Thanks to advancements in technology, embedded reporters were able to provide unprecedented coverage of a major war, including live images of U.S. forces engaged in actual combat. From the opening and much-hyped "shock and awe" bombing campaign to the fall of Baghdad, the reporting of the U.S. forces was mostly favorable.[1] Even though the coverage was considered to be objective, it was quick to provide us heroes, including a soldier who happened to be at the wrong place at the wrong time after her convoy took a wrong turn.[2]

The media was also used to support American information operations. Media reports of the awesome might and quick advance of the U.S.-led coalition is believed to have undermined Iraqi resistance.[3] Embeds confirmed the perfidious acts committed by surrendering Iraqi forces

---

[1] For the purposes of this article, the term "media" is used to denote a wide range of media and media organizations, including, but not limited to, producers, reporters, journalists, crews, production teams, headquarters staff, etc. Additionally, for consistency, this article focuses on the U.S. use of media in Operation IRAQI FREEDOM. The focus on the United States is not intended to demean or exclude the contributions made by the myriad other coalition partners. Finally, the term "information leveraging" is used to encompass both "information operations" and "public affairs," which doctrinally is excluded from the scope of the former.

and so effectively exposed the falsehood of the claims made by Iraqi Information Minister, Mohammed Saeed al-Sahhaf, aka Baghdad Bob, that he soon became fodder for political cartoons and late night television monologues. In short, the U.S. military effectively used the media to gain information superiority.

The thesis of this article is that modern media should be considered a legitimate military target under the law of armed conflict because it effectively contributes to military action and provides a direct advantage to combatants engaged in modern warfare. Using OIF as the primary case study and applying the law of armed conflict as interpreted by the United States, this article will examine what the embedded media enabled the U.S. armed forces to accomplish and why this now makes the media a military objective that can be targeted. At first glance, the logic of examining the U.S. use of the U.S. media may seem confusing as the United States, of course, would not attack the very media that contributed to U.S. military action. However, as today's practice will become tomorrow's precedent, understanding how the United States interprets international law can be useful in identifying potential vulnerabilities in future conflicts and enable operational commanders to study means to defend or minimize those vulnerabilities, especially for future wars in which the United States may encounter an adversary with better information-leveraging capabilities than that of the Iraqis.

BACKGROUND

US Military-Media Relations Through Operation Desert Storm

Reporters have long accompanied the U.S. armed forces into the battle space.[4] However, their conflicting missions and goals have resulted in a strained relationship.[5] During World War

II and Korean War, reporters accompanied U.S. combat units in the field, including all major operations and overall enjoyed a good working relationship.[6] The relationship changed during the Vietnam War with a breakdown of trust between these two institutions.[7] Enjoying unprecedented access to the battle space and the U.S. armed forces, the media began questioning the official reports provided by military spokesmen because they often painted a different situation than what they were observing.[8] The media began filing more negative reports about the war.[9] Eventually, public support for the war evaporated, causing many in the military, including many officers who would rise to leadership positions within the Department of Defense (DOD) in the 1980s and 1990s, to blame the media for the loss.[10]

The consequence was an attempt to stem the media flow of information during combat operations. For example, no reporters were allowed to be present during the 1983 Operation URGENT FURY on the island of Grenada.[11] A press pool was activated for Operation JUST CAUSE in 1989, but was delayed from getting to the battlefield until after combat had ended.[12] During Operation DESERT STORM, DOD was successful in implementing some extensive controls on the media, including press pools and reservation of the right to censor material.[13] For example, of the 1600 reporters in Saudi Arabia, only 186 were accredited to be in escorted pools accompanying the troops.[14]

Media Coverage in Desert Storm & Origins of Information Operations

Nonetheless, via Cable News Network (CNN) live broadcasts from Baghdad, "unilateral" media representatives who disregarded DOD rules, and DOD's own press conferences (complete with video of smart bombs hitting their targets) made media coverage of Operation DESERT

STORM a watershed event, both for the media and DOD.[15] For DOD, it demonstrated that the modern media could be employed to support important objectives, including mobilization of domestic and international support,[16] influencing the perceptions of the adversary's leadership,[17] and as a source of intelligence.[18] It also showed that our adversaries could likewise effectively exploit the media to counter these objectives, namely through the spread of disinformation or portraying coalition forces as indiscriminately targeting civilians and civilian objects.[19] The lesson learned was that in modern warfare the side that controlled the flow of information better was going to win the conflict.[20]

The result was the development of doctrine centering on the leveraging of information to influence the perceptions and decision-making by our adversary's leadership. Although primarily concerned with information operations, public affairs (PA) also was recognized as a capability to influence perceptions and affect-decision making by facilitating the flow of accurate and timely information, especially in countering an adversary's deception and propaganda.[21] It also creates awareness of military goals during a campaign, keep audiences informed, and allow a joint force commander (JFC) to inform an adversary about his force's intent and capability.[22]

Embedding

In October 2002, Secretary of Defense Rumsfeld announced that reporters would be permitted to accompany American combat units in the event of war with Iraq.[23] The guidance subsequently issued to all military commanders made it clear that, consistent with operational security considerations, they were to cooperate and accommodate the military in executing their mission of covering combat operations.[24] For the media, this course change was unexpected, but

4

welcomed.[25] His decision, however, had as much to do with waging war in the information age as it did with accommodating the fourth estate.

The Law of Armed Conflict[26]

The law of armed conflict is "the body of norms regulating the conduct of states and combatants engaged in armed hostilities."[27] It is based upon two equally compelling considerations: military necessity and humanitarian considerations.[28] However, it is not intended to impede the waging of hostilities, but to ensure that the violence of hostilities is directed toward the enemy's forces and not to cause wanton, unnecessary human suffering and needless destruction.[29]

The law of armed conflict is generally derived from two sources: international agreements and from customary international law.[30] The former includes the Geneva Conventions and treaties by which nations agree to perform or refrain from performing certain acts.[31] The second source consists of those practices that have attained "a degree of regularity and is accompanied by the general conviction among nations that behavior in conformity with the practice is obligatory"[32] and therefore considered binding on all states. Many of these customs have subsequently been codified in international agreements. This is the case with many of the fundamental targeting principles, which have been included in Protocol I.[33] Although the United States is not a party to these protocols, it is bound to those provisions to the extent Protocol I codifies customary international law.[34]

The law of targeting is based upon fundamental principles of the law of armed conflict, including the principle of distinction, which requires combatants to "distinguish between the civilian population and combatants and between civilian objects and military objectives" and direct their operations only against military objectives."[35] Article 52(2) of Protocol I defines "military objectives" as

> Those objects, which by their nature, location, purpose, or use, make an effective contribution to military action and whose total or partial destruction, capture or neutralization, in the circumstances ruling at the time, offers a definite military advantage.[36]

The relatively ambiguous definition of military objectives is intentional. Previous attempts to specifically delineate what constitute a "military objective" were destined to fail for incompleteness on account of the ever-changing nature of warfare.[37] Accordingly, the rule is couched as a two-prong test to be applied by a military commander when determining whether to conduct an attack. First, the object, whether by its nature, location, purpose, or use makes an "effective contribution to military action." Second, under the circumstances at the time, the commander must determine that its destruction, capture or neutralization would offer "a definite military advantage." The commentary to the rule does not define these criteria other than to state that "it would be inappropriate to launch an attack that offers only potential or indeterminate advantages" and "a definite military advantage" is very similar to terms used elsewhere in the Protocol, such as "concrete and direct military advantage anticipated."[38]

Finally, until Protocol I, there were no specific provisions addressing targeting of journalists. Article 79, Protocol I, provides that "[j]ournalists engaged in dangerous professional missions in areas of armed conflict shall be considered as civilians within the meaning of Article

50. paragraph 1" and "shall be protected . . . provided that they take no action adversely affecting their status as civilians."[39]

ANALYSIS

What Embeds Brought to the Fight

In OIF, approximately 777 journalists embedded with American combat units generated as many as 6,000 stories a week.[40] A Rand study concluded that the embedded media program can be viewed as "widely successful across a broad range of outcomes and measures."[41] It specifically listed the following positive military outcomes: generally maintained operational security during major combat operations phase; enabled the U.S. Government to fulfill its legal obligations regarding press access; built the credibility of the military; obtained good public relations; and supported information operations.[42]

The study's discussion on establishing good public relations and building of credibility were viewed as important successes in positive domestic public support for the war. The study concluded the embedded media program when coupled to the quick decisive victory, and the overall exemplary behavior of U.S. forces resulted in generally favorable reports filed by the media, which in turn led to sustained public support.[43] Additionally, because of the presence of embeds, Central Command spokespersons were careful to put out accurate information and qualify less certain reports, thereby establishing its credibility as honest, which further contributed to favorable public relations.[44]

The DOD PA officials who oversaw the embedded media program also understood the positive public relations dividend. In post-conflict assessments, they repeatedly pointed that these reporters enabled international audiences to see the U.S. military in "a very real and compelling way," including the "care they took to preserve innocent life" and "to minimize collateral damage."[45] Their repeated emphasis on these talking points made it clear that favorable public relations were a key objective of the embedded media program.

The study listed two examples of embedded media supporting "honest" information operations. First "the 'shock and awe' campaign at the beginning of the war made the press a willing participant in showing the advancing might of the U.S. armed forces," and noted that "while this display did not result in complete Iraqi submission, it likely had some effect, although this is difficult to measure."[46] Moreover, the media was used effectively to counter the misinformation put out by the Iraqi Minister of Information.[47] Again, this study confirmed the assessments of DOD PA officials, who stated that the embedded reporters showed the horrors and the atrocities of the Iraqi regime by reporting on the perfidious acts committed by Iraqi forces.[48] Most importantly, embedded reporters were instrumental in providing information assurance:

> We also knew, though, that our potential adversary . . . was a practiced liar, a person who used denial and deception and disinformation on a regular basis. And we knew we would want to try to counter and mitigate some of the effects of that constant flow of disinformation. And what better way to do that than with trained observers, kind of the definition of a reporter, out there in the field, able to report in near real time everything that was occurring as opposed to giving any credibility or credence to what the Iraq Defense Ministry might be putting out.[49]

Thus, as viewed by DOD and an independent research think tank, the embedded media program is viewed as having been successful in building domestic public support for the war effort, is believed to have undermined Iraqi will to fight, and was instrumental in countering Iraqi disinformation, which likewise contributes to building or negating public support. However, for the media to be targeted as a military objective, it must have "effectively contributed to military action" and constituted "a distinct military advantage" to the United States. An understanding of what war is and an examination of customary international law shows that the morale of the enemy, which includes that of the civilian populace, has long been considered a legitimate objective to be attacked in war.

What is War?

Carl von Clausewitz wrote that war was "a true political instrument, a continuation of political intercourse, carried on with other means."[50] He recognized that it involved more than the interaction of two armed forces, stating "when whole communities go to war—whole peoples, and especially *civilized* peoples—the reason always lies in some political situation, and the occasion is always due to some political object."[51] Thus, war between two armed forces involves entire nations, or "the remarkable trinity of war," consisting of the people, the government, and the military.[52] Victory was achieved by maintaining equilibrium of one's own trinity while disrupting the balance of the adversary's trinity by attacking on or more of the components.[53] As the origins of law of armed conflict predate Clausewitz, he was not advocating physical attacks against an enemy's civilian populace, but by bringing the war home to them so that the cost of obtaining the political object of the war becomes more expensive than its projected benefit. The trinity has been equated to "enemy morale," which has long been considered a legitimate objective for targeting.[54]

U.S. Interpretation and Application of the Law of Targeting

An examination of the targeting practices of nations throughout the twentieth century shows that enemy morale, including that of the civilian populace, was considered a legitimate objective of aerial bombardment.[55] In both world wars, nations with air power conducted bombing campaigns for the specific purpose of demoralizing their enemies to facilitate their respective wills to resist.[56] In Korea and Vietnam, the United States also conducted bombing operations for psychological advantages, including pressuring the North Vietnamese back to the bargaining table in the latter conflict.[57] As a corollary, the April 1942 raid on Japan by Colonel Doolittle was of little military value and was conducted mainly for boosting the morale of the military forces and the U.S. population.[58]

Doctrinally, the United States has also traditionally taken a more holistic approach to targeting. Current Air Force doctrine maintains that air power is not solely for destroying purely military targets.[59] The USAF Intelligence Targeting Guidance and Joint Publication 3-60 reference the language of Article 52(2) as a starting point, but focus of the strategic necessity of the target, rather than its military characteristics.[60] These targeting publications are in consonance with Navy guidance on targeting that likewise defines military objectives as those objects that contributes to the enemy's war-fighting or war-sustaining capability.[61]

Finally, there is a precedent for bombing a media outlet because of its content. On 23 April 1999, while supporting North Atlantic Treaty Organization's (NATO) Operation ALLIED FORCE, U.S. missiles struck the downtown Belgrade studios of Serbian-owned radio and television station, killing sixteen civilians and injuring another sixteen persons.[62] The attack was preceded by a general warning to western media outlets by NATO around 12 April 1999 that the studios could be attacked. NATO formerly justified the attacks on the grounds that intelligence had determined that it had been integrated with that government's strategic and operational command and control (C2) structure.[63] However, comments by a NATO spokesman also indicated that the attacks had been executed because the studios were used for the generating of propaganda, making it a legitimate target under the law of armed conflict.[64]

These statements resulted in accusations by the non-governmental organizations, Human Rights Watch (HRW) and Amnesty International (AI), that NATO had committed war crimes.[65] Their investigations resulted in the establishment of a committee by the prosecutor to the international criminal tribunal for Yugoslavia (ICTY) to review the NATO bombings.[66] The interpretations of military objective offered by these organizations and accepted by the ICTY demonstrate the potential political ramifications that JFC can face, especially when operating in an effects-based environment.

HRW recognized that "stopping such propaganda may serve to demoralize the Yugoslav population and undermine the government's political support,"[67] but argued this purpose did not qualify it as a legitimate military target because it did not constitute a concrete and direct military advantage. AI condemned this attack on the grounds that eliminating a civilian facility used for propaganda purposes stretched the "the meaning of 'effective contribution to military action' and 'definite military advantage' beyond the acceptable bounds of interpretation." [68] The ICTY Committee concurred, concluding that although NATO had demonstrated sufficiently that the studios were being used for C2 purposes, the facility nonetheless did not constitute a military objective:

> As a bottom line, civilians, civilian objects, and civilian morale as such are not legitimate military objectives. The media does have an effect on civilian morale. If that effect is merely to foster support for the war effort, the media is not a legitimate military objective. If the media is used to incite crimes, as in Rwanda, it becomes a military objective. If the media is the nerve center that keeps a war-monger in power and thus perpetuates the war effort, it may fall within the definition of a legitimate target.[69]

The Committee concluded that disrupting government propaganda for purpose of disrupting the morale of the population and the armed forces did not meet the "effective contribution to military action" and "definite military advantages" criteria as "defined" under Article 52(2) of the Additional Protocol to make the civilian station a military objective.[70]

These narrow interpretations demonstrate an ignorance of Clausewitz's teachings and the realities of war. War is not fought in a vacuum. The remarkable trinity still remains an important objective in defeating one's enemy. Military planners often include it as a center of gravity. Maintaining domestic public support remains an important objective in war.

General Wesley Clark, USA, who was the NATO Supreme Allied Commander during Operation ALLIED FORCE, had no qualms about attacking the station solely on the grounds that it was a propaganda machine. Reflecting on how Yugoslav President Slobodan Milosevic used the media in an effort to undermine the collective will of the NATO alliance, General Clark wrote:

> The Serbs . . . were excellent in organizing press coverage and directing it toward NATO mistakes. From the outset we had seen that the Serbs would do all they could to portray the NATO strikes as targeting civilians, rather than Serb military and police. . . . The fact was, the Serbs were on the ground and we weren't. They had an immediate advantage in knowing what happened when the bombs struck and, when the result was embarrassing to NATO, they could assure world media coverage faster than we could investigate and explain it.[71]

In other words, because he was unable to defeat NATO through the use of force, he attempted to undermine the credibility and the political will of the alliance. Through the selected use of factual information–public affairs–Milosevic was able to portray NATO as engaging in the indiscriminate killing of civilians and civilian objects. This put NATO on the defensive, requiring its leadership to spend days explaining and clarifying the events while Serbs continued to commit atrocities out of the cameras' reach.[72]

The Impact of Modern Media Provides a Definite Military Advantage

The most important compelling attributes of the modern media which makes it useful to combatants in achieving their operational objectives are that its ubiquity, continuity, and immediacy. These characteristics are what enable it to impact (but not necessarily lead or direct) the manner in which foreign relations are conducted, including hostilities.[73] That is, with its ability to broadcast in real time from anywhere around the world, twenty-four hours a day, the media effects immediate public awareness of world events. This immediacy prevents political and military leaders to "get out ahead of the problem," thus requiring them to operate in a more reactive manner. Because of the twenty-four hour news cycle, nations now must seek to influence within the news cycle.[74] Accordingly, this is what makes countering disinformation an important objective in modern warfare. If left unchecked, disinformation can effectively frustrate national strategic, theater-specific, and operational objectives. Thus, when Baghdad Bob stood in front of the world's television cameras that the Americans were being slaughtered and nowhere near the Iraqi capital, the media's split screen video of Marine tanks rumbling through the crowded Baghdad streets were able to effectively prove the falsity of his statement more powerfully than anyone at Central Command Headquarters could. In short, the media does matter to governments in the information age as it informs the populace and an informed populace is more apt to make itself heard.

Even the anticipated public reaction to news can impact decisions. Towards the end of Operation DESERT STORM, U.S. jets relentlessly attacked an Iraqi convoy withdrawing from Kuwait City. In the end, 1,400 vehicles, only of which twenty-eight were either tanks or armed personnel carriers, had been destroyed along a two-mile section of highway.[75] An estimated two to three hundred dead Iraqi soldiers were determined to have been killed in the attacks.[76] When the media arrived on scene a few days later, it began broadcasting images of this scene from what it quickly captioned as the "Highway of Death." Concerned that these images would undermine American public for the war, President George H. W. Bush and Chairman of the Joint Chiefs of Staff, General Colin Powell, directed General Schwarzkopf to end the war before all objectives, including the destruction of the Iraqi Republican Guard, had been achieved. [77]

A World With No Embeds

Up to this point, this author has tried to show through circumstantial evidence how the modern media makes an effective contribution to military action and provides a definite military advantage. This has been done this by discussing U.S. interpretation of international law, the precedent set by the United States in the bombing of Radio Television Serbia (RTS) Studios in 1999, and discussing the impact of the media in the information age, and discussing the advantages that DOD and Rand researchers believed the embedded media brought to the U.S. military in OIF. Part of the problem in examining the principle of the military objective in the OIF context is the lack of post-conflict evidence gathered from Iraqis that would confirm the U.S. perceived effectiveness of the information operations that it conducted. To the author's knowledge, there has been no strategic survey conducted in Iraq as there was in Japan following the end of World War II. Nonetheless, anecdotal evidence may demonstrate the military advantage provided to the United States by embedded media. In this case, it is what has happened during the post-hostilities phase:

> With the fall of Baghdad and Saddam's regime, embedded reporters left the front and returned home to news stories. By the end of April 2003 less than 40 embedded reporters remained in Iraq. With their departure, the military lost the ability to leverage the media. They no longer

14

enjoyed information superiority. With the loss of embeds, there were too few public affairs officers in the stabilization force to ensure the remaining reporters, now based in Baghdad hotels, covered the good news stories (previously observed by embedded reporters). Charged with getting a story to lead the hourly news coverage, the reporters concentrated on sensational stories of ambushes and riots/looting/sabotage vice stories of schools opening, water or power restoration. etc.[78]

Polling data may provide some merit to this assertion. During the combat phase of OIF, in March 2003, an American Broadcasting Company/Washington Post polls showed that 64-71 percent of persons polled approved of the way President Bush was handling the situation with Iraq.[79] A CBS News poll found that as many as 80% of persons polled approved of the United States taking military action against Iraq to try to remove Saddam Hussein from power.[80] In the post hostilities phase, these approval ratings were below 50%.[81] Although other reasons factor into these low numbers, including the lack of weapons of mass destruction, the constant negative reporting out of Iraq undoubtedly is also a factor.

"THANKS JAG, BUT WHAT DOES IT ALL MEAN?" (RECOMMENDATIONS)

Having a working knowledge of the law of armed conflict assists the operational commander in identifying potential vulnerabilities and likely enemy courses of action. While this is less true to the asymmetrical groups the United States is currently facing in the Global War on Terrorism, most nation-states are more likely to comply with the law of armed conflict because of the possible negative implications that result from breaching its provisions.[82]

Yet the broad interpretation afforded to the term "military objective" by the United States in its targeting doctrine and practice nonetheless raises a concern that these interpretations could be used against us in justifying attacks on "our" media. Attacks on individual news media representatives in the battle space is not the concern; not only would targeting them not disrupt our ability to leverage information, but most nations who have ratified Protocol I have agreed not

15

to do so. Disruption of U.S. information leveraging would require neutralization of the media's transmission and broadcasting capabilities. A strike on CNN Headquarters by an enemy who had the capacity to penetrate our homeland defenses in a time of war is unlikely. However, such a scenario does raise questions about our assumption that the United States will always have the media to exploit in achieving information superiority. It is an assumption that is based upon the large size and ubiquitous nature of the U.S. media enterprise. Nonetheless, the consequences of a partial or total destruction of the media should be considered with contingency plans formulated for ensuring the United States is able to maintain the flow of information.

Shifting focus, the proposition that the media constitutes a legitimate military target also has important implications for the JFC who is responsible for all aspects of the targeting process, including the establishment of objectives.[83] As the doctrine of effects-based targeting continues to mature, it is likely that the destruction or neutralization of media and media infrastructure used for producing propaganda may be identified as an objective that will lead to achievement of operational objectives. Under U.S. interpretation of international law, this is a legitimate military target. However, before doing so, the JFC should review the following considerations in an attempt to minimize the political backlash that occurred following Operation ALLIED FORCE.

First, determine if the desired effects can be achieved by alternative means. In Kosovo, the radio transmitter towers were originally targeted for destruction.[84] However, this eventually migrated to the studios themselves because it was assessed that it was the critical node that, if destroyed, would permanently degrade Milosevic's C2 apparatus. In fact, the television and radio stations were back on the air within hours after the attack.[85]

16

Second, if a strike on a civilian media facility is deemed necessary, provide advanced warning to the extent possible to minimize civilian casualties.[86] Again, in Kosovo, NATO issued a broad warning to western media that the studios were targeted, but specified no period of time as to when it may be struck. Although this warning was deemed sufficient by the ICTY Committee and understanding the need for operational security, providing a more direct warning after you have gained air superiority (if not dominance) would further minimize civilian casualties and the international scrutiny that will surely follow.

CONCLUSION

In the information age, war continues to be an act of force to compel an adversary to comply with specific requirements. The difference today is that the media not only reports, but is used by adversaries to disrupt the equilibrium of their respective opponents' triangle to achieve strategic and operational objectives. Accordingly, under U.S. interpretation and application of the law of armed conflict, this use of the media brings it within the definition of "military objective," making it susceptible to attack. Understanding this, military commanders may lawfully target media infrastructure, but should do so only as a last resort and even then, providing advance warning to the extent possible without jeopardizing mission success or operational security. Finally, recognition that the U.S. position is a double-edge sword, which may be used against us, should cause operational commanders to identify what vulnerabilities attacks on U.S. media would cause to his ability to conduct information operations.

[1] Christopher Paul and James J. Kim, *Reporters on the Battlefield: The Embedded Press System in Historical Context* (Santa Monica: Rand Corporation, 2004), xvii-xx.

[2] Ibid., 112-113.

[3] Ibid., 83.

[4] Herbert Sparrow, "The Military Versus the Media," in *The Media and the Gulf War*, ed. Hedrick Smith (Washington D.C.: Seven Locks Press, 1992), 63.

[5] Many have attributed their uneasy relationship on the account of their separate culture and objectives, such as the military's desire for operational security versus the media's goal to report on newsworthy information. Christopher Paul and James J. Kim, *Reporters on the Battlefield*, 26-28. Bernard E. Trainor, "The Military and the Media: A Troubled Embrace" in *The Media and the Gulf War*, 69-80.

[6] Herbert Sparrow, "The Military Versus the Media," in *The Media and the Gulf War*, 64-65.

[7] Christopher Paul and James J. Kim, *Reporters on the Battlefield*, 36-37.

[8] Ibid.

[9] Ibid.

[10] Ibid., 38.

[11] Ibid., 39-40. An anecdote displays the lack of affection between the military and the media: Some reporters did attempt to reach the island via speedboat, but turned back after US fighter jet fired two sets of warning shots across their bow. Later, one of the reporters asked the task force commander, Vice Admiral Joseph Metcalf what would have happened had happened if they had not turned around. Without skipping a beat, Metcalf responded, "We would have blown your ass right out of the water." H. Norman Schwarzkopf. *It Doesn't Take A Hero: The Autobiography* (New York: Bantam Books, 1992), 257-258.

[12] Christopher Paul and James J. Kim, *Reporters on the Battlefield*, 40-42.

[13] Ibid., 42-45.

[14] Ibid.

[15] Ibid. *See, also,* Thomas B. Allen, F. Clifton Berry and Norman Polmar, *CNN: War in the Gulf: From the Invasion of Kuwait to the Day of Victory and Beyond* (Atlanta: Turner Publishing, Inc., 1991), 232.

[16] Christopher Paul and James J. Kim, *Reporters on the Battlefield*, 42-45.

[17] General Schwarzkopf recounts a September 1990 press conference that was being broadcast internationally in which he was asked if it was true the United States was still weeks away from being able to defend against a ground attack. "I gave the strongest answer I could: 'If the Iraqis are dumb enough to attack, they are going to pay a terrible price.' With those cameras grinding away, I knew I wasn't just talking to friendly audiences, but that Saddam and his bully boys were watching me on CNN in their headquarters. I wanted to make sure they got the message." H. Norman Schwarzkopf. *It Doesn't Take A Hero*, 344-45.

[18] B. Allen, F. Clifton Berry and Norman Polmar, *CNN: War in the Gulf*, 236.

[19] For example, US Air Force F-117s struck the Al Firdos bunker on February 13, 1991. Intelligence assessed it to be a command and control facility. However, it actually was an air-raid shelter. Hundreds of civilians sheltered there were killed. The Iraqi regime quickly ushered news crews there to record the carnage. In the immediate aftermath, US officials blamed Iraqi leadership for using the civilians as human shields and argued they were to blame for the carnage. Post-war analysis would confirm that it was an air raid shelter and not a C2 facility. Michael R. Gordon and Bernard E. Trainor. *The General's War: The Inside Story of the Conflict in the Gulf* (Boston: Little, Brown and Company, 1995) 324-327.

[20] Joint Command and Control & Information Warfare Staff, Joint Forces Staff College, *Information Operations: The Hard Reality of Soft Power* (Norfolk, VA: National Defense University, 2002), 10 [hereinafter "JCC&IWS, *Information Operations*"].

[21] Information operations (IO) are defined as "[a]ctions taken to affect adversary information and information systems while defending one's own information and information systems." The five pillars of IO are considered operational security, psychological operations, military deception, electronic warfare, and computer network attack/defense. Ibid. PA is considered an activity related to, but not part of, IO. Joint Chiefs of Staff, *Joint Doctrine for Information Operations*, Joint Pub 3-13 (Washington, DC: 9 October 1998), viii, GL-7. Joint Chiefs of Staff, *Doctrine for Public Affairs in Joint Operations* (Washington, DC: 14 May 1997).

[22] Joint Chiefs of Staff, *Joint Doctrine for Information Operations*, II-6.

[23] Bill Katovsky and Timothy Carlson, *Embedded* (Guilford, CT: The Lyons Press, 2003), xiii.

[24] This guidance included access to operational combat missions, space on military transportation, logistical assistance, no outright ban on communications equipment, and no review process. DOD, *Public Affairs Guidance*.

[25] Bill Katovsky and Timothy Carlson, *Embedded*, xiii. DOD had actually embedded media with combat units in Bosnia and Haiti, but not of the magnitude of OIF. Christopher Paul and James J. Kim, *Reporters on the Battlefield*, 47-49.

[26] The law of armed conflict is synonymous with the law of war and international humanitarian law. It should not, however, be confused with human rights law. As explained by the International Committee for the Red Cross, "International humanitarian law and international human rights law are complementary. Both seek to protect the individual, though they do so in different circumstances and in different ways. Humanitarian law applies in situations of armed conflict, whereas human rights, or at least some of them, protect the individual at all times, in war and peace alike. While the purpose of humanitarian law is to protect victims by endeavouring to limit the suffering caused by war, human rights seek to protect the individual and further his development." As quoted by Charles Garraway, "*Ius In Bello*: Law of Armed Conflict" (PowerPoint presentation presented to the elective course in Operational and International Law Issues for Commanders at the Naval War College in September 2004), in possession of this article's author.

[27] Matthew C. Waxman, *International Law and the Politics of Urban Air Operations* (Santa Monica, CA: Rand, Inc., 2000), 5.

[28] Charles Garraway, "*Ius In Bello*."

[29] Department of the Navy, Office of the Chief of Naval Operations, and Headquarters, US Marine Corps. And Department of Transportation, US Coast Guard, The *Commander's Handbook on the Law of Naval Operations* (Norfolk, VA: Naval Doctrine Command, 1995), 5-1 [Hereinafter "DON, *The Commander's Handbook*"].

[30] Ibid. 5-2.

[31] Ibid.

[32] Ibid.

[33] Protocol Additional to the Geneva Conventions of 12 August 1949, and Relating to the Protection of International Armed Conflicts, *opened for signature* Dec. 12, 1977. http://www.icrc.org/ihl.nsf/ 7c4d08d9b287a42 141256 739003e636b/f6c8b9fee14a77fdc12564 1e0052b079 [14 February 2005].

[34] The United States has not ratified the additional protocols. Although it recognizes many of the provisions codified in Protocol I, it does not concur with the narrow interpretations of the rules. Horace B. Robertson Jr., "The Principle of the Military Objective in the Law of Armed Conflict," *United States Air Force Academy Journal of Legal Studies* 8 (1997), 35.

[35] Protocol I, Article 48. The principles of distinction and the prohibition against causing unnecessary suffering to combatants have been described as the "cardinal principles" of the law of armed conflict. Horace B. Robertson, Jr., The Principle of the Military Objective in the Law of Armed Conflict," 40.

[36] Protocol I, Article 52. Subparagraph one of this article defines civilian objects as all objects which are not military objectives. Ibid., at Article 52(1).

[37] Claude Pilloud, et al, *Commentary on the Additional Protocols of 8 June 1977 to the Geneva Conventions of 12 August 1949*, ed. Yves Sandoz, Christophe Swinarski, and Bruno Zimmermann (Geneva: Martinus Nijhoff Publishers, 1987), 630-633 [hereinafter "Piloud, et al, *Commentary on the Additional Protocols*"].

[38] Ibid., 636-637.

[39] Protocol I, Article 79.

[40] Katherine M. Skiba, "Journalists Embodied Realities of War," *Milwaukee Journal Sentinel*, 14 September 2003, p. 01J. The number of reporters who registered and who actually accompanied US forces in the field vary. The Rand Study put the number of actual embeds at over 600. Christopher Paul and James J. Kim, *Reporters on the Battlefield*, xiii.

[41] Christopher Paul and James J. Kim, *Reporters on the Battlefield*, xvii.

[42] Ibid.

[43] Ibid.

[44] Ibid., xviii.

[45] Department of Defense, Office of Assistant Secretary of Defense (Public Affairs), *Deputy Assistant Secretary Whitman Interview with NPR* [transcript], (Washington, D.C.: 2003); available from http://www.defenselink.mil/transcripts/2003/tr20030425-0150.html; Internet: accessed 5 December 2004 [hereinafter "DOD, ASD(PA), *Deputy Assistant Secretary Whitman Interview*].

[46] Christopher Paul and James J. Kim, *Reporters on the Battlefield*, xviii.

[47] Ibid.

[48] Doug Hanolen, "Q & A: The Pentagon Experiment; Spokeswoman Clarke Deconstructs Embed Process," *Television Week* [database online], 19 May 2003; available from www.lexis.com; Internet; accessed 14 February 2005.

[49] DOD, ASD(PA), *Deputy Assistant Secretary Whitman Interview*.

[50] Carl von Clausewitz, *On War* trans. and ed. Michael Howard and Peter Paret (Princeton, NJ): Princeton University Press, 1976), 87.

[51] Ibid., 86.

[52] Ibid., 89.

[53] Ibid.

[54] Jeanne M. Meyer, "Tearing Down the Façade: A Critical Look at the Current Law on Targeting the Will of the Enemy and Air Force Doctrine," *The Air Force Law Review* 51 (2001), 143-182.

[55] Ibid.

[56] Ibid., 154-160.

[57] Ibid., 168.

[58] Ibid., 169.

[59] Ibid., 171-172, quoted the 1997 version of AFDD-1, which has been superseded by Department of the Air Force, *Air Force Doctrine Document I: Air Force Basic Doctrine*, AFDD-1 (Washington, DC: 17 November 2003). The pertinent sections quoted by the author were as follows:

> War is an instrument of national policy. Victory in war is not measured by casualties inflicted, battles won or lost, or territory occupied, but by whether or not political objectives (one's own and those of the enemy) shape the scope and intensity of war. Military objectives and operations must support political objectives . . .

> War is a clash of opposing wills . . . . While physical factors are crucial to war, the national will and the leadership's will are also critical components of war. The will to prosecute or the will to resist can be decisive elements.

> [Strategic] operations are designed to achieve their objectives without first having to necessarily engage the adversary's fielded military forces in extended operations at the operational and tactical levels of war . . . . Strategic attack objectives often include producing effects to demoralize the enemy's leadership, military forces, and population, thus affecting an adversary's capability to continue the conflict.

[60] Both define military objective to include objects that make and effective contribution to the military capability of the adversary. Ibid., 172. Joint Chiefs of Staff, *Joint Doctrine for Targeting*, Joint Pub 3-60 (Washington, DC: 17 January 2002), A-3.

[61] DON, *The Commander's Handbook*, 8-1.

[62] International Criminal Tribunal for the Former Yugoslavia (ICTY), "Final Report to the Prosecutor by the Committee Established to Review the NATO Bombing Campaign Against the Federal Republic of Yugoslavia," *United Nations Press Releases* 13 June 2000. < www.un.org/icty/pressreal/nato061300.htm> [16 December 2004] at paragraph 9 [hereinafter "ICTY Report"].

[63] Ibid. Connected to more than a hundred relay stations in Yugoslavia, NATO intelligence had determined the studios had been incorporated into the government's strategic and operation command and control structure, with military traffic being routed through it and the station's equipment having been used to support the activities of the Former Republic of Yugoslavia military and special police forces. Frederic L. Borch, "Targeting After Kosovo: Has the Law Changed for Strike Planners?," Naval War College Review (Spring 2003) ___ .

[64] NATO spokesman Jamie Shea explained the attack on the studios as follows: "We had nothing against the media, but RTS is not media. It's full of government employees who are paid to produce propaganda and lies. To call it media is totally misleading. Its function is not to produce news and information; its function is to incite hatred and to distort reality, not to reflect reality, but to distort it. And therefore, we see that as a military target. It is the same thing as a military propaganda machine integrated into the armed forces. We would never target legitimate, free media. Let me make that point clear. But please, and I'm sure you're not doing this, do not confuse RTS with CNN Center in Atlanta, or BBC Milbank House, or La Masion De La Radio in Paris. They don't have anything at all in common." "Targeting Serb TV," Newshour with Jim Lehrer [transcript] 23 April 1999. < http://www.pbs.org/ newshour/bb/europe/jan-june99/serb_tv_4-23.html> [14 February 2005].

[65] Jeanne M. Meyer, "Tearing Down the Façade," 165.

[66] ICTY Report, ¶ 7.

[67] Jeanne M. Meyer, "Tearing Down the Façade," 165.

[68] Ibid.

[69] ICTY Report, ¶ 55.

[70] Ibid., ¶ 76.

[71] Wesley K. Clark, *Waging Modern War* (New York: Public Affairs, 2001), 443.

[72] Ibid.

[73] Department of Defense, Office of the Under Secretary of Defense for Acquisition, Technology, and Logistics. *Report of the Defense Science Board Task Force on Strategic Communication.* (Washington, DC: 2004), 11-20.

[74] "The effects of technology and the 24-hour news cycle should not be underestimated. Coverage provided by the embedded press, together with increases in other forms of media coverage, can exaggerate both good and bad news. Increased coverage makes information available to the public that had previously been available only to military personnel, in some cases resulting on political and military authorities to respond more quickly in the past. This is a real concern for decision makers and field commanders alike and may not serve the public interest." Ibid., xxii.

[75] Michael R. Gordon and Bernard E. Trainor. *The General's War*, 370.

[76] Ibid.

[77] Ibid., 415, 418, 477. Schwarzkopf, *It Doesn't Take a Hero*, 542.

[78] Glenn T. Starnes, "Leveraging the Media: The Embedded Media Program in Operation Iraqi Freedom," *Student Issue Paper, Center for Strategic Leadership*, US Army War College, July 2004, Volume S04-06.

[79] Taken from a compilation of public opinions polls regarding U.S. involvement in Iraq available at <http://www.pollingreport.com/iraq.htm> [7 February 2005].

[80] Ibid.

[81] Ibid.

[82] The consequences of these breaches include diplomatic protests, reprisals and other enforcement actions. DON, *The Commander's Handbook*, 6-1.

[83] Joint Chiefs of Staff, *Joint Doctrine for Targeting*, Joint Pub 3-60. vii.

[84] ICTY Report, ¶ 76.

[85] Ibid., ¶ 78.

[86] Protocol I, Article 57(2) obligates combatants to mitigate civilian casualties by providing advance warning of impending attack.

Allen, Thomas B., F. Clifton Berry, and Norman Polmar. *CNN: War in the Gulf* Atlanta Turner Publishing, Inc., 1991.

Borch, Frederic L., "Targeting After Kosovo: Has the Law Changed for Strike Planners?" *Naval War College Review* Newport, RI: Spring 2003.

Clark, General Wesley K. *Waging Modern War.* New York: Public Affairs, 2001.

Department of Defense, Office of the Under Secretary of Defense for Acquisition, Technology, and Logistics. *Report of the Defense Science Board Task Force on Strategic Communication.* Washington, DC: 2004.

_____, Secretary of Defense, *Public Affairs Guidance (PAG) on Embedding Media During Possible Future Operations/Deployments in U.S. Central Commands (CENTCOM) Area of Responsibility,* SECDEF MSG 101900FEB03Z. Washington, DC: 2003.

Department of the Navy, Office of the Chief of Naval Operations, and Headquarters, U.S. Marine Corps, and Department of Transportation, U.S. Coast Guard. *The Commander's Handbook on the Law of Naval Operations.* Norfolk, VA: 1995.

Fialka, John J. *Hotel Warriors: Covering the Gulf War.* Washington DC: The Woodrow Wilson Center Press, 1991.

Gordon, Michael R., and Bernard E. Trainor. *The Generals' War: The Inside Story of the Conflict in the Gulf.* Boston: Little, Brown and Company, 1995.

Howard, Michael and Peter Paret, eds., *Carl Von Clausewitz: On War.* Princeton, NJ: 1976.

International Committee of Red Cross. Protocol Additional to the Geneva Conventions of 12 August 1949, and Relating to the Protection of International Armed Conflicts, *opened for signature* Dec. 12, 1977.

International Criminal Tribunal for the Former Yugoslavia. "Final Report to the Prosecutor by the Committee Established to Review the NATO Bombing Campaign Against the Federal Republic of Yugoslavia." *United Nations Press Releases.* 13 June 2000 http://www.un.org/pressreal/nato061300.htm [16 December 2004].

Joint Chiefs of Staff, *Doctrine for Public Affairs in Joint Operations,* Joint Pub 3-61. Washington, DC: 14 May 1997.

_____, *Joint Doctrine for Information Operations,* Joint Pub 3-13. Washington DC: 9 October 1998

_____, *Joint Doctrine for Targeting*, Joint Pub 3-60. Washington, DC: 17 January 2002.

Joint Command and Control and Information Warfare Staff, *Information Operations: The Hard Reality of Soft Power*. Norfolk, VA: 2002.

Katovsky, William and Timothy Carlson. *Embedded: The Media at War in Iraq*. Guilford, CT: The Lyons Press, 2003.

Meyer, Jeanne M. "Tearing Down the Façade: A Critical Look at the Current Law on Targeting the Will of the Enemy and Air Force Doctrine." *The Air Force Law Review* (2001).

Paul, Christopher and James J. Kim. *Reporters on the Battlefield: The Embedded Press System in Historical Context*. Santa Monica, CA: Rand Corporation, 2004.

Pilloud, Claude. *Commentary on the Additional Protocols of 8 June 1977 to the Geneva Conventions of 12 August 1949*, ed. Yves Sandoz, Christophe Swinarski, and Bruno Zimmermann Geneva: Martinus Nijhoff Publishers, 1987.

Robertson, Jr., Horace B. "The Principle of the Military Objective in the Law of Armed Conflict," United *States Air Force Academy Journal of Legal Studies* 8. Colorado Springs, CO, 1997.

Schwarzkopf, H. Norman. *It Doesn't Take a Hero: The Autobiography*. New York: Bantam Books, 1992.

Smith, Hedrick, ed., *The Media and the Gulf War*. Washington, DC: Seven Locks Press, 1992.

Starnes, Glenn T. "Leveraging the Media: The Embedded Media Program in Operation Iraqi Freedom." *Student Issue Paper, Center for Strategic Leadership*. Carlisle, PA: July 2004.

Taylor, Philip M. *War and the Media: Propaganda and Persuasion in the Gulf War*. Manchester: Manchester University Press, 1992.

Waxman, Matthew C. *International Law and the Politics of Urban Air Operations*. Santa Monica, CA: 2000.

Woodward, Bob. *The Commanders*. New York: Simon and Schuster, 1991.